MAGIC
MAIZE

by
Mary and Conrad Buff

HOUGHTON MIFFLIN COMPANY BOSTON
The Riverside Press Cambridge

PROLOGUE

The land of the Maya
A land of cool highlands
A land of hot jungles
A bountiful land

Years ere Columbus
Sailed the Atlantic
The Maya built cities
Of richly carved buildings
Of temples colossal

From the sun and the moon
From the stars in the sky
They learned of the seasons
The time to plant maize
The time of its harvest

Thus grew noble cities
Thus bloomed giant temples
And greater spread knowledge
As year followed year

Then kings, priests and nobles
Strong—ever stronger
Quarreled and hated
Fearing each other

Came intrigues and hatreds
Then wars never-ceasing
Crushing the cities
Wasting the maize fields
Burying all knowledge
Forgotten forever

The land of the Maya
A land of cool highlands
A land of hot jungles
A bountiful land

CONTENTS

CHAPTER ONE

BURNING THE FIELD

FABIAN, the Indian boy, awakened as something crawled over his face. He brushed it away. Half awake, he wondered if a scorpion had crept from under his sleeping mat. Scorpions were poisonous. He sat up, blinking his eyes. Then he saw a frayed string dangling above him. It was the string that tied Chichi, the parrot, to her perch. That had awakened him. So Chichi had flown away again. She must have cut the string with her sharp bill.

The boy jumped quietly to his feet. He saw his father praying at the family altar, a rickety table. A candle lit up Father's sad face, wrinkled by years of hard work in the hot sun of Guatemala. Fabian heard a soft "pit-a-pat" as his mother patted dough thinner and thinner between her brown hands. He had heard this sound

1

as long as he could remember. As Mother watched the tortillas bubble on the griddle Fabian slipped out of the smoky hut. He must find that naughty Chichi.

It was windy outside. Pigs were squealing and turkeys were gobbling. Hens cackled. Was a coyote lurking about? In the gray light of early dawn the boy noticed that the gate of the pigpen was ajar. It must have blown open during the night. Then he saw Chichi in the pen. She was fighting mad. As baby pigs milled about her trying to grab a kernel of maize she nipped them with her sharp bill. Two black vultures were fighting for food too. "Get out, get out," shouted Fabian, picking up a rock and throwing it at the vultures. The great birds swooped upward, alighting on the thatched hut. They perched there looking like two mourners at a funeral, for they were pure black. Fabian grabbed the bit of string still tied to the parrot's scaly leg and pulled her up to him. She clung to an outstretched finger. Then the boy closed the gate of the pen and tiptoed quietly back into the smoky hut.

Father was still praying. Fabian tied the parrot to her perch with a stronger piece of fiber. Then as she coughed just as Father always coughed, Mother glanced up from her cooking and said, "Oh, Fabian, you're awake at last. Here, eat these tortillas while they are still hot." Fabian crouched beside the tiny fire flickering between three black rocks. He was thinking of his parrot that Quin, his older brother, had brought from the hot jungle where parrots lived. Chichi had many tricks. She cried just like Fernando, the baby, so Mother was never quite sure if Fernando or Chichi cried. Father complained that Chichi chattered much too much. Often when a friend came to see him the bird would scream, "Get out,

get out," and that was not polite. Tsnuk, Fabian's older sister, was sometimes angry at Chichi too. The parrot would cackle exactly like a laying hen but when Tsnuk looked for an egg there was no egg.

Still thinking of Chichi, Fabian ate one, two, three, four, five, six crisp tortillas, followed by a steaming gourd full of black beans. "Are you not sleepy this morning, Mother?" he asked politely as his mother yawned. "You were awake all night."

"Yes, but we will sleep well tonight, son. One MUST do this each year before the field is burned. That is the custom." She spoke as if Fabian did not know this ancient custom of the Indians. He too had been awake most of the night listening to the prayers, the stories and the songs of his parents and visiting neighbors.

"Fabian, cut a leaf from the banana tree outside," asked Mother. The boy took a long shining machete from his sash and stepped outside. He cut a firm leaf from the graceful tree and handed it to Mother. He watched her as she cut the leaf into nine squares. Then she poured the hot corn mush into the squares and wrapped each one, tying it with fiber. "Put these in your bag, son," she said; "they are food for the Wind Gods and the Gods of the Field."

Father had finished his prayers. He stood up, and raising a heavy hoe to his shoulders said, "Fabian, it is time to go to the field. I will carry the nine gourds." Silently father and son walked down the rocky trail to the shores of the great lake. They untied a dugout canoe and paddled across a narrow inlet to the farther shore. The two climbed upward along a trail made smooth by the bare feet of many Indians. Above loomed a great brown volcano,

on whose slopes the Indians planted their maize. As they reached their weed-covered field bounded by a stone wall, Fabian could scarcely see the volcano, for smoke from burning fields swirled about its crest.

It is the custom in Guatemala for Indians early each year before the rains fall to burn last year's brush from their fields. As this was a windy morning many farmers were burning weeds. The Mayan boy gazing upward at the great mound of earth asked, "Father, have you ever felt the earth tremble and seen fire leap from the mouth of the volcano?"

"No, son," answered the father, "but Kiskin, God of the Underworld, is not dead, he only sleeps."

"Will he wake up someday, Father? Do you think he will?" asked Fabian.

"I do not know, son, I, nor any man, when Kiskin will awaken. But when he does he will shake our village to pieces as a dog shakes a rat. But I hope not in my time nor in yours either, Fabian. Still, one never knows."

Fabian looked at the ring of volcanoes around the lake, blurred by the smoke of brush fires. But he did not think too much about Kiskin, the God of the Underworld. He knew that his father was always fearing something. The Moon and the Sun were gods. There were gods in rocks, trees, hills, water, sky. Father prayed to all of them. He followed the old customs faithfully.

"Son," the father said, "place the nine gourds in a row. Put mush in each one. I will make a cross." As he said this he found two sticks and pushed the longer one into the earth, tying the shorter one across the first. Then as the sun rose, Father said,

"Fabian, as I pray to the Gods of the Wind, listen well and remember. Someday you too will stand in your own field and your son will stand beside you. You will pray as I am praying and he will learn from you."

Father prayed to the Wind Gods who guarded the four sides of his field. He begged them to blow hard so that the fire would burn all the brush. He asked the spirit owners of his field to eat the good mush in the gourds. He begged them to protect his future crop from drought, flood and disease. He gave them this good food and he expected them to repay him with kindness. Then father and son lay in the shade of a small tree and waited for the Spirits of the Field to eat. Fabian watched the colors of the lake change as waves rose in the rising wind. He watched the smoke curl upward into the sky from the Indian fires. He thought, How did man ever get fire in the first place? When man found fire, if it ever went out, how did he ever make it again? Thinking about this he asked, "Father, did people ALWAYS have fire?"

Father was quiet for a few moments as if he were trying to remember something. He pulled his straw hat over his eyes to protect them from the bright sun. Then he answered, "There must have been fire in the beginning, son. For when I was a boy my father told me an old story. Perhaps I can remember most of it."

Fabian sighed and settled himself in the dust and waited. Somehow he knew that Father was in the mood for storytelling. "A long, long time ago," began Father, "our people lost fire. I don't know how. Perhaps someone who should have cared for it fell asleep and forgot to feed it. So it died. Of course when fire was dead no one knew just how to make it live again. So our priest sent two men across the lake in a dugout canoe to ask the people over there to give us some of their fire, for they had it. But the people who lived on the other side of the lake were ancient enemies and they only threw rocks at the messengers.

"When the two men returned the priest decided to try another plan. He asked the people to bring their finest weavings, their best maize, and colored feather headdresses. Then, putting these gifts into the canoe, he sent the messengers across the lake once more. But again they were driven away by rocks and arrows, and returned without fire. So the priest talked with the elders and they decided to steal fire if they could not get it any other way."

"How did they do that, Father?" asked Fabian.

"It was very simple," continued Father. "The head priest called his faithful black dog to him. He commanded the dog to swim the lake that night with a candle in his mouth. When the dog reached the other side, he crept to a fire and lit the candle. No one saw him, for all the people were asleep. The dog slipped away in

the darkness and swam the lake. When he reached home the candle still burned. That was the way we fooled our enemies and got fire again."

Fabian laughed as he said, "I'll tell that tonight to Tsnuk and Caterina as we lie on our sleeping mats." Thinking of his sisters led him to think of Quin, his sixteen-year-old brother, who was a peddler and traveled from village to village. "Father," he asked, "why does Quin stay away from home all the time? He could help us in the field if he were here. The work is hard. He is so strong."

Father's tired face grew stern as he said, "Quin was always a strange boy. Even when he was little he was always running away from home. Then when he was your age his godfather once took him to Solola to the great market. When Quin came home he talked much about the wonderful things he had seen."

"What did he see, Father?" asked Fabian eagerly.

"I can't remember now, it was years ago," answered Father. "Perhaps he saw monkeys and iguanas, the great reptiles from the jungle, new fruits he had never seen, and of course all kinds of people who dressed and spoke differently from us. He saw fire-works and a church procession. Anyway, after that he always wanted to go with Godfather. Now that he is a man he has become a peddler and goes everywhere. From the jungle to the highlands, to near markets and to far markets he goes, always carrying something to sell on his back."

"Do you sometimes wish he were at home, Father?"

"Yes, I do, Fabian. The eldest son SHOULD help his father. That is the custom," he said bitterly. "But if Quin wanders about like a monkey and will not stay at home and help in the field, then

he will not. But enough of this son, enough! Let us light the fires now. The Gods have eaten."

Fabian could see how angry the thought of Quin made his father, so he said nothing more. He lit a pile of dry weeds with a match. The wind blew gustily. As flames spread, the Indians piled weeds upon weeds. Raking, cutting, hoeing, they spread the fires all over the field as smoke rose in the air. Fabian's throat soon became dry. His white shirt clung to his sweating back. The weeds slowly burned down to piles of gray ashes. Fabian thought of pleasant things like cool water, Chichi, black beans in a gourd, oranges. Then the boy knelt to pull out a stubborn stalk. He felt something round and hard. He clasped it and drew it from the dusty earth. It was a clay pot. It had many small holes in it. "Father," he called, "Father, look what I have found!"

Father, gray with dust, stumbled toward Fabian. When he saw the pot he exclaimed, "Son, that is a pot of the ancients, used for steaming maize. Only, one handle is gone. It must have rolled down long ago from the CITY UP YONDER in a storm. He looked upward to the slope of the volcano where lay the ruins of an old Mayan city. "This has been a good day, son," said Father, now smiling. "The Wind Gods liked the mush, for the field burned well. This pot we will place on the altar beside the twin ear of

maize from last year's crop. The blessed Mother of God will be pleased. Surely the harvest this year will be good."

Shouldering their hoes, the Indians hastened down the trail and paddled across the inlet, eager for water and food. "After we eat, son, we will heat the rocks in the Ika and throw water on them. We will cleanse ourselves together. The field was dusty."

Fabian thought to himself, Father must be pleased. He has asked me to bathe in the sweat house with him. Perhaps the old pot has made him happy. Maybe some day he will love Quin too. Father is so sure he is always right. Fabian sometimes wondered if there were not other ways to be right than just Father's way.

CHAPTER TWO

THE MAGIC MAIZE

WE are going to the mountain cave, children, to sacrifice a turkey to the Gods and pray for a good crop. The way is long. We will not return until tomorrow," said Mother, tucking sleepy Fernando in her carrying shawl. "There is much for you to do while we are away."

Father slipped his black and white bag over his shoulder, picked up a white turkey by the legs, and shouldered a burden containing food for the journey as he said, "Fabian, you and the girls shell all the maize hanging from the roof before we return. Put all the little kernels in that brown jar. Mother will use them for tortillas. But be careful and put all of the big ones in the basket and keep the lid on. Don't let Chichi eat them. Those we will plant."

"Yes, Father," answered the children dutifully. Fabian wished he could play all day long. He might rope baby pigs. He might go hunting with the dog Balaam, or he could play ball. Now he had to work. But as Father's word was always law he only said, "Yes, Father."

"Girls," Mother added as she turned to go, "be sure and throw water on the tomatoes this afternoon. They are dry."

"Yes, Mother," said Tsnuk who was in charge of the tiny plot of early tomatoes by the lake. The children watched their parents

trotting along the dusty trail to the mountains as long as they could still see Mother's bright red skirt. Husband and wife always went together to pray at mountain shrines. It was thought that a man's prayers would not be answered if his wife did not pray with him. Fabian leaned lazily against the doorway, listening to quarreling pigs and noisy turkeys. He watched two black vultures glide from the crest of the hut, where they usually roosted, as an avocado dropped to the ground from a tall tree. In but a moment the birds had cleaned the avocado of its meat, leaving only an empty shell.

"Fabian, don't stand there daydreaming. You heard what Father said," scolded Tsnuk. "Pull down that maize from the roof so we can get to work." She spread a straw mat on the dirt floor of the hut as Fabian piled three wooden boxes one upon another. He climbed up on them and tore down ears of maize which had hung from the rafters all year to dry. They were the biggest and the very best of last year's crop. The children sat on the floor and began to husk the corn. Some of the kernels were black, others yellow and others dark red like all Indian corn.

"Caterina, don't throw those little kernels there," scolded Tsnuk. "Put them in the brown jar as Father said. We don't plant those."

Caterina was only five years old and so did not always understand things. The leaves of the banana trees outside the open door crackled in the wind. From far off came the sound of Indians playing flutes. The children watched the pile of colored maize in the basket grow higher. Chichi chuckled just like Father when he heard a joke. Then she cried for a while like Fernando and finished

her morning song by gobbling like a turkey. How she would have liked to jump with both feet into the basket of colored maize, but the string on her leg kept her from moving far. Then, because the morning was warm, she fell asleep.

Finally Fabian said, "The day we burned the brush in the field, Tsnuk, Father told me an old story about fire. Have you ever heard it?"

"Yes, Mother knows it too; she told it to me. About the black dog?"

"Yes, the black dog," answered Fabian.

Gazing at the pile of maize growing ever higher, Tsnuk said, "I heard a new story from Godmother, about how man got maize. Ever heard that?"

"No, tell it while we work. Then the time will go faster," said Fabian, always ready for a story.

"It's about ants, little ants in the forest, and the animals," added Tsnuk.

"Ants," chimed in Caterina, "there's lots and lots of ants under the coffee bushes and in the pigpen."

"Not those ants, baby," said Tsnuk, wise in her ten years.

"Well, go on," added Fabian impatiently.

"Well," drawled Tsnuk, "a long time ago people didn't have any maize at all. They ate roots they dug out of the ground and coyotes and rabbits and jaguars they killed with bows and arrows."

"Where was all the maize then?" asked Fabian.

"Under a big rock in the jungle," the girl continued. "No one knew about it but the ants. But one day a fox was hunting near the rock and he saw seeds on the ground. The ants had dropped them

when they came out of a crack in the rock. The fox licked up the
seeds and liked them. So being a smart fox, he waited and more
ants came out of the crack and dropped seeds. He licked up those
kernels too and the more he ate the more he wanted. That night
he went back into the forest. The other animals smelled something
sweet on his breath and asked, "What have you been eating, Fox?"

"Nothing," said the fox, "just bananas like the ones you eat."

But as the jaguar smelled the fox's breath he said, "He has
not been eating bananas. That's a new smell."

The fox only grinned, showing all his white teeth. But the
other animals did not trust him, for he was a tricky animal. That
night as he slipped away from the others they followed him
silently. When the fox stopped at the rock, they hid behind trees
and bushes. Then as they saw him licking up something from the
ground, they rushed out and jeered at him.

"Did they like the kernels of maize too?" asked Fabian.

"Of course they did. They all liked them," said Tsnuk. "And they all waited at the rock every night. When the ants came out with the maize, the animals made them drop the kernels and licked them all up. But soon there was not enough maize for all of the animals. So they tried to dig under the rock but it was too big. Then they decided to ask the Gods, the Mams, to help them. The Mams were so strong. They hurled thunderbolts at the rock, but could not break it. It was very hard."

"It must have been," said Fabian. "What did they do then?"

"Well, the Mams had to go to the greatest Mam of all, Yaluk. 'You are so very strong, Yaluk,' they said. 'There is a new food we all like under a big rock. It is very good to eat. But only you are strong enough to break the rock with your thunderbolts. Won't you break the rock for us and for the animals of the forest?'

"Yaluk was a wise old Mam. He knew that the other Mams had already tried to break the rock and had failed. He just yawned and said wearily, 'I'm getting to be an old man now, and not as strong as I once was. Just look at my arm. Like an old grandfather's.'

"He was just teasing the others, of course. But that night he said to Woodpecker, 'You tap the rock all over and find the weakest place.' The woodpecker did and Yaluk said, 'Now get out of sight. Hide! I will hurl a terrible thunderbolt. If you look you will get hurt.'

"The woodpecker was curious as he always is, and he did stick out his head to see what Yaluk was doing. A rock hit him on the head and made it bleed. That is why all the woodpeckers now have red heads."

Fabian laughed at the thought of the curious woodpecker.

"Well," continued the girl, "the thunderbolt was so terrible that even old Yaluk fainted dead away. While he was asleep, the other Mams grabbed all of the white maize kernels, and ran away and planted them. But Yaluk, when he came alive again, found

only yellow, black and red kernels of maize. But he planted these anyway and you know how well they grow. That is our Indian corn."

"That's better than the fire story," sighed Fabian. "I will remember to tell Agustín about it when he comes next." Agustín was Fabian's very best friend.

"Oh, Agustín goes to school and maybe he won't believe the story," said Tsnuk.

Fabian smiled as he answered, "Maybe he won't believe it, but he will like it anyway, for it's a good story."

Just then the church bell tolled in the distant village church. It was midday.

"I'm hungry," whined Caterina. Tsnuk handed her a basket of cold tortillas.

"Caterina," commanded Tsnuk, "remember Mother told us to water the tomatoes. Let's go now, and maybe we can wash our hair and skirts in the lake afterward." The girls took their brown water jars from a bench and soon were out of sight. Fabian continued to shell the last of the ears of maize. The day was sunny and warm. He looked out of the open door. In the far distance he saw the tiny figure of a peddler, *cascate* on back, plodding toward him in the dust. Then he heard the dog Balaam bark far away. He knew that bark. Balaam knew the peddler. Fabian watched. Soon he saw that the distant peddler was none other than Quin, his dear older brother. He jumped up and ran to meet his brother, crying, "Quin, how good to see you home again."

Quin grinned happily, his teeth very white in his brown face. He took off his hat, and slipped the heavy wooden *cascate* from his back to the ground. Fabian carried it into the cool hut. As they entered, Chichi screamed, "Get out, gringo, get out." The two brothers laughed as Quin said, "Don't you remember me any more, Chichi? And you traveled with me for months, too." Chichi chuckled. Then turning to Fabian, Quin asked, "Where are the girls and Mother and Father?"

"The girls are at the lake watering the tomatoes. Father and Mother went early this morning to the mountain cave to pray for a good crop. They will not be back until tomorrow."

"That's a lot of maize you have been shelling," said Quin looking at the pile of kernels in the basket.

"Yes, we plant soon. We have shelled all morning," added Fabian.

"That makes me remember, little brother, I have something for you," said Quin, opening his black and white bag and taking out a banana-leaf package. "Here, Fabian, look at these."

In the green package lay a few silky, white kernels of maize. Fabian looked at his brother with wonder in his eyes as he asked, "But Quin, we have much maize to plant; why do you give me these when the basket is full?"

"Just because, little brother, this is a new kind of maize. It is not like that in the basket. The gringos have made it from our own maize, somehow, I don't know how. But anyway it grows well. Big and strong, and each kernel alike. No little ones."

At the word gringos, Fabian felt like throwing the seed to the pigs. He knew his father would never let him plant any maize that came from gringos, the "white people." They were foreigners and not to be trusted. And so he asked, "Where did you get these kernels of maize, brother, and why do you want to give them to me?"

"Listen, little brother, I will tell you how I got the twenty kernels. Last year I was going to a market high in the mountains with a heavy load of bananas. I wished to get to the village market very early, for then I might sell all of my bananas. So I took an

old trail I had walked before. It made the village many miles nearer. The rain was falling in torrents. It was hard to see. The trail was slippery. Many times I wished I had taken the longer but safer road. But I had gone so far then that it was not worth while to go back.

"I reached a curve in the trail. The rain was coming down so hard I could not see a foot in front of me. Suddenly I slipped, fell and rolled down the hill. Every time I tried to get up the wooden *cascate* of bananas was on top of me. I cried out. Then I heard someone answer. Suddenly a man helped me to my feet and dragged me to the trail."

"Who was it, Quin?" asked Fabian.

"Listen, I'll tell you. It seems that part of the trail had completely washed away. I could see nothing because of the rain. But I was not hurt. I looked up, for the man was taller than I. I saw a fellow with a huge black beard. He spoke Spanish. He was a gringo. 'Are you hurt?' he asked.

" 'No,' I said in Spanish, 'but I lost many bananas.'

" 'We will help you,' he answered. Another man came. He was very white and had a red beard. Then came an Indian from the village of Andreas. He knew not only Spanish but a few words of our language. It was still raining. The men led me to a camp, where they were living in tents."

Fabian listened eagerly. He loved to hear his brother tell of faraway places and strange peoples. "What then, Quin?" he asked.

"Well, after a while the rain stopped. You know how quickly it begins and how quickly it ends. The two men asked me to stay and talk with them and get dry. I had never known such kind people

before. I thought all gringos were evil. The black-bearded man was from Mexico and his name was Gómez. The very white man was from a land farther away. I think his name was Señor Johnson. Well, I stayed all night with the gringos. It was a wonderful night. We sat around the fire and the gringos gave me much to eat. Some of it was meat out of cans. It was very good. Then we talked. The men had been digging in the earth for weeks. In this spot were pyramids, old tombs, ruined buildings. It was something like the CITY UP YONDER only much larger. The men were digging for things made by our forefathers, the Maya. They told me many stories of the Dawn People."

"What did they tell you, brother? I want to know."

"So many things I can't remember all of them. They said our forefathers were a great people. They knew more about the stars, the moon and sun, and when to plant and harvest maize than any people that had ever lived. They built beautiful cities years and years ago. They had no horses for the Spaniards brought them to

this land many years later. They did not know about the wheel. So all the pyramids and cities and temples were built by slaves who carried rocks and trees on their backs for miles and miles. It was wonderful to hear these gringos tell of our people. I was proud of our race. When morning came and I was ready to go, the white man helped find the bananas I had lost, or at least some of them. And they bought some from me too and I went on to the village very happy. But the last thing I told them before I left was where I lived, on the shores of this great lake. Also I told them of the CITY UP YONDER. If they should ever want to dig there, I said, perhaps my brother, Fabian, would guide them to the ruins, for he knew the ruins well."

"Oh," was all that Fabian could say, he was so excited.

"But Quin, what did the men find in the ruins on the mountain? You have not told me."

"Oh just some things our people had made long ago. A dagger, I remember, all carved, with a black blade and very sharp. Many green beads of jade. A figure of the Maize Goddess. They hoped to find more things of jade, which was used only by priests and kings, but they did not. Jade is rare you know.

"Just before I left," Quin continued, "the men shook hands with me, *me,* a poor Indian peddler. Then Gómez said, 'Take these twenty kernels of new seed, Quin. It is the maize that we are planting in our country. It grows better than the old Indian maize. Even if we made it, it is good, Quin,' and as he said this he smiled. 'Take it with you and somewhere you will meet a farmer who will plant it. Some day it will be planted all over your country, and there will be more tortillas for your people. It is the seed of the future.'

"So I took it, little brother, and there it lies in your hand. Let's call it the Magic Maize."

"Yes," agreed Fabian, staring down at the silky kernels in

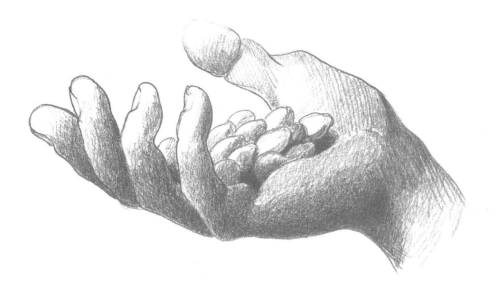

his brown hand, "we shall call it the Magic Maize." Then his face saddened as he said, "But Quin, if Father sees this he will never let me plant it, especially if he knows the maize came from the gringos. He will throw it to the chickens."

"He might," answered Quin, "but why does he need to know? You plant it in some secret place. When the plants are tall and full of ears, then is the time to show Father, not now," added his wise, elder brother.

"But you know how Father is," protested Fabian. "He does not like it that you are away from home. He does not like it that you do not believe the old myths and legends. He spoke of you the day we burned the field on the volcano. He was very sad and angry too."

"I know, I know," answered Quin, "but I see many things as I carry bananas from the jungles to the highlands and maize from the highlands to the jungle. I have known many kinds of people, Fabian, and now I know that they are much alike. Whether they are Indians or gringos they are alike. Some are good, others are bad. But most of them are neither all good nor all bad. It is easy to see why Father hates the gringos. The Spaniards were cruel to the Indians for as long as anyone can remember. But those days are going."

Fabian said nothing. He was already wondering where he could plant the silky maize. "Are you staying all night, Quin?" he asked at last.

"No, I must buy some chick-peas in the market and then take the boat and cross the lake. Early in the morning I must be in Solola for the market. But tell Mother and Father all is well."

Quin shouldered his heavy burden and smiled as he said, "I am going now, brother. Remember the shut mouth catches no flies." Chichi seemed to know that Quin was going, for she said, "Get out, get out of here." Balaam the dog followed him as he took the dusty trail to the village.

As the sun set behind the dark volcano the girls returned, their hair still wet, their red skirts clinging to their brown limbs. Tsnuk built a fire between the three black rocks as Fabian fed the pigs and the turkeys. Great clouds glowed in the west as the sun set. The lake was red like blood. The chickens chattered from their safe perches in the trees. The candle on the altar flickered in the evening wind as the sweet face of the Holy Mother smiled from her place of honor. Fireflies flickered in the sudden darkness. Fabian felt at peace. The magic maize was sleeping in his treasure bag. It had been a wonderful day. Perhaps Father and Mother would be pleased at all the work they had done and take them to the next market. And that was something to look forward to.

CHAPTER THREE

PLANTING

FABIAN kept his treasures in a white woolen bag that he had knitted and decorated with rows and rows of black horses. This was his dearest possession which he kept hidden under his sleeping mat. In the bag he had three green jade beads and two red and blue feathers Agustín said were from the tail of the quetzal bird, the national bird of his land. The quetzal bird roamed only in the forests, and was rare and shy. Into the bag now went the twenty seeds of new maize—also a jaguar's tooth. In May, when the rains fell, he would find some secret place to plant the magic corn.

The boy had not long to wait. In April Father took the twin ear of maize that had rested all winter on the altar and carried it to church, together with some maize seed. He burned a candle to

Saint Santiago and prayed that the twin ear would inspire the new seed. When he came home Godfather and Godmother were there and the family prayed, talked, ate and drank all the night through. The next day was planting day.

After breakfast Mother again wrapped mush in nine pieces of banana leaf. Before dawn Fabian and his father rowed across the inlet and climbed to their field. Father placed the gourds in a row as Fabian slid the mush into each one. Now they waited for the Rain Gods, and Che, the guardian of the field, to eat.

"When will we be through planting, Father?" asked the son.

"It may take us twelve days if we work hard. The earth is dry and we must plant deep," said Father. "There is little maize left in the granary. If this year's crop is no better than last year's we may have to pick coffee berries for Señor Schulz if we are to eat at all."

"But Father, the tomatoes are ripe now and the pigs are getting big. We will sell them and the turkeys."

"Yes, of course we will sell them, Fabian, and Mother's weaving, too, at the market, but still we must have maize to eat. Each day maize. We cannot live without maize."

Fabian thought about this as he watched the lake, now turning deep blue. Dugout canoes from the village labored across the water. He heard a distant chug-chug as a small motor launch plowed its noisy way to a distant hamlet. At last his father said, "The gods have eaten. Let us plant now." He raised his heavy hoe and dug a hole as deep as the length of a man's hand. Fabian dropped five kernels of maize into the hole with seeds of squash and beans. All of the morning back and forth across the field the two worked. The sun was hot. Sweat poured down Fabian's face.

He worked steadily on, trying to keep up with Father. Not once did he complain of the dust or the heat. He dropped the red, black and yellow kernels of maize into the holes. Toward noon great clouds rose and hid the sun. The mounds of earth made a pattern of tiny hills across the brown land. Finally Father wiped his face with his sleeve, pulled off his straw hat and leaning wearily on his hoe said, "When one has not slept one's old bones are as water. Let us go home, son. We have done well."

Tired, hungry and thirsty, they stumbled down the hill. As Fabian passed one Indian field after another, he wondered just where he could find a place to plant his magic seed. All of the land was in use. "When I am a man, Father," he asked finally, "may I have a little part of our field for my very own?"

"That will be a long time, Fabian," replied his father. "You must know the prayers to the gods and all about planting and harvesting first."

"But Agustín is only a little older than I am and he has a piece of his father's field already. He goes to school too."

"School, school, school! I hear nothing else," stormed his father. "That is a place where boys learn to play. I became a farmer without going to school and so shall you."

Fabian did not reply. There was nothing to say. One obeyed one's father. But Agustín had told him of the many things he had learned at school. Fabian was sure he did not play all of the time. As Father and son rowed across the narrow inlet toward home, a motorboat passed. On the roof were burdens of pottery, mats, chickens, maize and fruit. The launch bulged with Indians. A few white people, gringos, sat on chairs at one end of the boat separated from the Indians. When Father saw them he turned his head away, for he did not even like to see the gringos. Father feared all gringos.

Just as Fabian reached home he saw Agustín, his best friend, waiting for him. He whispered, "Agustín, wait for me at the corner

of the compound. I have something to tell you." When he had hung up his hoe Fabian rushed out to see his friend. They walked away from the hut and Fabian said very quietly, "When Quin was here he gave me twenty kernels of a new maize; he called it magic."

"Why magic?" asked Agustín. "Was it blessed by the priest or the medicine man?"

"Oh no, not that kind of magic," replied Fabian. "It came from the white people far away. It grows better than our Indian seed."

"Have you planted it yet?" queried Agustín.

"No, not yet. I wonder where I can. If Father knew it came from the gringos he would feed it to the pigs. You know how he feels about anything new, especially from far away and from strangers."

"Yes, I know," laughed his friend, "he thinks all gringos are evil." He was quiet for a moment and then he said, "I have an idea. There is a little place near the CITY UP YONDER where we could plant the seed. Nobody would go there."

"I thought you would know of some place," said Fabian, happy now. "When shall we go and plant it?"

"Tomorrow night? I can meet you at the lake when the sun goes down. The moon will be up later. It will be light enough to see," whispered Fabian's friend.

"I will meet you," was all that Fabian said as Agustín slipped quietly away.

CHAPTER FOUR

THE MARKET

FABIAN stared out of the door at the long-awaited rain. It poured down in a gray sheet. A streak of lightning cut the dark clouds above the volcano. It was very early morning.

"The Rain Gods are whipping their horses," said Tsnuk gravely, watching the lightning and listening to the thunder. She was sitting on the dirt floor stringing up a strap loom just like Mother's.

"It's good Father and I put new thatch on the roof," grinned Fabian. "See, not a drop of water has seeped through yet." A sudden crash of thunder and some more lightning. "The Rain Gods are felling the trees with their bows and arrows. Hear them!" whispered Tsnuk to her sister, Caterina. Caterina was frightened.

The children were all alone in the hut, for their mother and father had gone to call upon Godfather, who was sick. Fabian watched the stiff leaves of a banana tree whip against the wall in the wind and break into strips. Chichi croaked sadly on her perch. She did not like the rain.

"How are you, Chichi?" asked Fabian, petting her smooth, silky feathers.

"Got a cold, got a cold," she croaked, blinking her wise eyes, for she was almost forty years old. Then she twisted about on her perch and called sweetly to Balaam the dog, "Come here, friend, come here, friend, come here, friend."

Poor Balaam could never resist a kind word from anyone. He was always fooled by Chichi's loving voice. He slunk to her and nosed her long tail feathers. Then, as suddenly as the lightning, she nipped his tail with her sharp bill. Balaam yelped and limped back into his dark corner, licking his bleeding tail.

"He never, never learns," said Tsnuk sadly, "he just never learns."

"Chichi, why do you tease Balaam like that, you naughty parrot?"

But Chichi only chuckled and muttered sadly to herself. "I got a cold, I got a cold." Then she cried just like the baby.

"Just for that you don't get any of my tortilla," scolded Tsnuk. "You know better, Chichi." But Chichi did not mind what anyone said. She just closed her eyes and dozed on her perch.

Then suddenly, as if someone had pulled away a gray curtain from the sky, the sun appeared. The earth steamed. Everything looked fresh and green.

"Mother said if the rain stopped we might go to the market in the village. This is market day," said Fabian hopefully. Almost as if Mother had heard him, the parents appeared suddenly. Father was smiling. He was happy over the first rain.

"Get ready, children, we can go to market," said Mother also smiling. "Girls, hurry down and pick the tomatoes that are ripe." The girls hurried off. Mother rolled two sashes she had woven and thrust them in her bag. Fabian went to the pigpen and selected the three largest pigs. Then he tied a string about their legs, and stood ready for the family to come. Soon they were all jogging along on the trail. Fabian was far ahead, trying to keep up with the pigs.

Many Indians were on the trail. Each little girl looked just like her mother, for she was dressed the same. Each boy was dressed like his father. Everyone carried something to sell. The women carried huge baskets on their heads. Often a turkey or a hen lay inside the basket, or a pile of fruit. Each man and boy carried something on his back.

When the family reached the market Mother found her own place. It was the same place her family had used for years. She paid but a few cents rental each week for it. Tsnuk held the scales, made of two woven baskets on a rod, as Mother arranged the tomatoes, keeping a tin box in her sash in which she kept change. Baby Fernando slept cozily on her back.

"Fabian," said Father, "I am going to the church to burn a candle and to pray for a good crop. You take the pigs to the animal market. Wait for me there. It is best to go around the market, for the pigs are lively and you might get into trouble."

It would have been better if Fabian had obeyed his father. But the great number of wonderful things to be seen was too tempting. He marched with his pigs between the aisles of sitting Indians, their little mounds of fruit and vegetables for sale on the ground before them. Bananas, oranges, avocados, piles of mangos. Chick-peas, garlic with braided stems from across the lake. Blankets from the higher lands. Candles, machetes, and bits of copal that the Indians burn for sacrifice. Ropes, red chests, mats to sleep on, mounds of black soap, hats of straw and of course high piles of water jars and pottery for cooking. It was all too exciting to miss.

All went well until the boy reached a peddler from the jungle, who wore about his middle a string of long, squirming lizards.

Fabian stood fascinated by these strange creatures, called iguanas, from the hot lands. They were just like the tiny lizards that played about his house, only giant-sized ones and therefore frightening. Perhaps the pigs were frightened too, for all at once they rushed in three different directions, squealing and pulling on their ropes. An old woman, heavily loaded with a basket of hens upon her head, stumbled over the tight ropes. Down she went, the chickens spilling from the basket, the woman falling into the dust. Just then the leash snapped on the leg of one of the pigs. Off he raced, squealing and darting between everybody's legs. What a riot!

Fabian tearfully helped the old woman to her feet, piled the hens in the basket and politely said he was sorry. Then he looked around for the escaped pig. Picking up the other two in his arms, he ran in the direction of the third pig. Just as he reached the animal market, he saw a boy about his age, holding the rascal in his arms. Thanking him, Fabian tied the fugitive again. Then he sat on a rock and fanned himself with his hat. He was very hot and tired, but relieved that he had caught the pig.

Before long Father arrived. "You may go now, son, and help your mother. When the church bells ring at midday I will meet you. If I have sold the pigs, that is," he added. Fabian was happy to be free. Now he could look at everything without pigs to get in his way. He followed a man with a canary in a cage, a fortune teller. The canary told fortunes by picking a tissue paper from a wheel with his bill and handing it to his master. When the master gave the customer the paper to read, usually everyone laughed. The fortune was always good.

When Fabian passed the little outdoor cafés, and smelled

the big pots full of boiling stew, he became very hungry. But it was not yet midday. So he listened to four men playing a marimba, an ancient instrument made of different-sized gourds. The music made him feel like dancing. At last the church bells boomed. It WAS midday. He hastened to find Mother's place. Half the tomatoes in the basket were sold. They were riper than the tomatoes in other baskets. Tsnuk weighed them out as Mother made change. Fabian saw the two sashes Mother had woven on the ground in front of the tomatoes. A white woman stopped to look at them. Mother waited and said nothing. As the woman still looked, Mother held them out to her. The woman asked in Spanish, "How much?"

Mother stared at her and then replied, "Three quetzales."

Fabian knew that the sashes were not worth that much. So did Mother. She waited quietly, expecting the woman to name a much lower price. But the gringa only laid down the sashes and began to walk away. Mother called out, "Two quetzales." Without a word the gringa picked up the sashes and handed Mother two quetzales. Nodding politely she said, "Adios," and walked away. Mother giggled. "How foolish these people are," she whispered to Tsnuk. "They will pay anything you ask. They do not bargain."

"Mother, give us some centavos, now you have so many," whined the children. Mother smiled and gave each child five centavos. "Get yourselves something to eat. But come back soon. We go home before long."

The market seemed to melt away. Peddlers were hastening to catch the afternoon boat. People were packing things on their

heads and backs. Soon the square would be empty. No one could imagine then that it had been full of people early in the morning.

The children hurried between the narrow aisles searching for a pink drink they loved. But Caterina wanted a piece of *panela*—brown sugar. Fabian gulped down his sweetish drink as he watched the people going home. Then he saw Father. Father must have sold the pigs, for he carried a roll of rope in his hand. It must be the rope to put around the field when the maize ripens, Fabian thought. It would have to be blessed by the medicine man and boiled in sacred things first. Then the coyotes and the deer and the dogs, too, would not eat the young ears of maize.

It was always good to wait till the end of the day to buy anything in the market. Things became cheaper. Now all of the tomatoes were sold. Mother bought a ball of black soap, some salt tied in a banana leaf and a new water jar. When she bought some stick cinnamon, Fabian knew that she would make a sweet drink he loved, flavored with cinnamon. Father had the shoemaker make him a pair of new sandals.

Before long everybody was tired. Fernando was crying. It was time to go home. Slowly Fabian trailed after his family as they made their way homeward. Clouds had arisen. "It will rain tomorrow," said Father happily.

CHAPTER FIVE

THE CITY UP YONDER

THAT night Fabian and Agustín met on the shore of the great lake. The moon was full and the water shone like a polished silver plate. The boys both had their long machetes in their sashes, for one never ventured into the jungle without a machete. One never knew what one might meet. Jaguars roamed there, and wolves and wild boars. But worse than any of the animals were the spirits of the other world. As they rowed the dugout canoe across the inlet they spoke together only in whispers. Tying the boat they crept silently along the trail toward the CITY UP YONDER. Fabian felt his bag often to be sure the magic maize was there.

At last, puffing and panting, they reached the place where once a great city stood in the days before the Spanish conquerors.

49

The last king of their tribe had fought his last battle at this place and had been killed. It was beautiful but frightening in the CITY UP YONDER. Scattered about were great dark boulders with strange figures carved upon them. Many of the figures were winged snakes. Some of the boulders had basins carved on their tops. The basins were in deep shadow and looked like dark pools.

"See those basins," said Agustín. "Once a long time ago maybe there was blood in them."

Fabian gulped as he thought of a basin of red blood. "They told us about that in school," continued Agustín. "In the days before the Spaniards, the priests held a prisoner of war over a rock like that. They slit the man's breast and tore out his still-beating heart. The blood poured into a bowl like that one there," he whispered, pointing to a near-by rock. "Sometimes the people drank the blood, for they thought it would make them strong and brave."

Fabian trembled. He was afraid of the rocky basins. Then they came upon a squat dark figure of an old Mayan idol. Both boys had seen black idols before, but in the moonlight and at the CITY UP YONDER it was terrifying. "Let's hurry and plant the maize, Agustín, and get back home," said Fabian hardly above a whisper.

"Over there is a good place by those trees. In the daytime the sun shines long here. I know," said Agustín who knew almost every foot of the CITY UP YONDER. Fabian dug a hole as Agustín dropped one white kernel of maize into it. "If we plant only one kernel in every hole and they all come up and grow, then Father MUST believe the seed is good. In our fields we plant four

or five kernels in every hole and sometimes none of them come up," whispered Fabian.

The boys were working hurriedly when suddenly Agustín muttered, "Fabian, listen. Do you hear something?"

"What?" asked Fabian, his heart beating fast.

"Something barking, just like a little dog, and not far away."

"What is that?" asked the younger boy, dropping his hoe. "Sounds like a *cuchito*."

At the word *cuchito,* Fabian trembled again. He stood as still as a stone idol, almost without breathing. But, as the minutes raced by, the barking grew fainter. Soon they could not hear it. "A *cuchito* barked all night once near our house not long ago," he said, "and Mother and Father did not sleep. Mother said the volcano might spurt out fire or the earth shake. Father believed someone in our house might get sick and die. But nothing happened."

The moon was high overhead now. Inspired by its silvery light a nightingale sang in the darkness of the trees. The lovely odor of a night-blooming flower added to the mystery of the tropical night. Glowworms winked here and there like lanterns going on and off. If he had not been at the CITY OF THE DEAD ONES, Fabian would have loved the warm, fragrant darkness, the sweetly singing bird and the odor of jungle flowers. But soon it seemed that everything about him grew dim and pale. The light of the moon was fading. When he looked into the sky and saw no cloud over the moon, he noticed that part of it was strangely in shadow.

"Agustín, look at the moon. It is growing smaller all the time. See that shadow moving across it. It is getting darker. Oh," he cried, "the moon is dying."

"We must get away from here," breathed Agustín, "something terrible is about to happen." He dug one hole after another and they dropped the last kernel of maize. Then, as Fabian knelt down to smooth the earth over the buried seed, he felt something smooth and round. He thought it was a worn stone. But as he held it up to the fading light of the dying moon, he saw it was dull green and was carved.

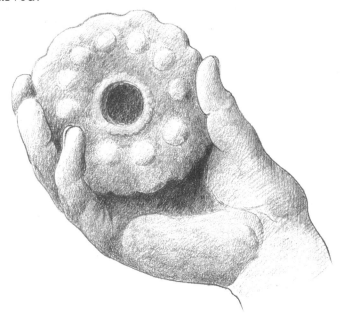

"Look, Agustín, what I have found. What is it?" he asked wonderingly.

"Oh, Fabian, that is an old, old earplug. Maybe the king wore that once, when he fell in battle, for it is jade. Maybe a high priest. I have seen pictures in a book at school," he said, polishing the green earplug on his shirt.

"That's almost as good as the pendant you found, Agustín, isn't it?" asked Fabian as he slipped the earplug into his shoulder bag.

"Maybe," answered his friend, "but let's get off this mountain. It's getting darker all the time." The boys ran down the trail, their machetes ready in their hands. When they heard the weird hoot of a hidden owl, they ran even faster. "They say the owl leads the jaguar to his prey, Fabian, so we'd better hurry," whispered Agustín.

The fireflies flickered in the darkness. Once Fabian stumbled and almost fell, but at last the frightened boys reached the canoe and paddled as fast as they could across the inlet. Then they heard the church bells pealing, and the noise of tin pans and drums being beaten. "Listen to the bells and the drums," they whispered to one another. "People in the village are scaring away the evil spirits who are stealing the light of the moon."

After they tied their canoe, they hurried up the hill and stood under the shade of the coffee bushes, watching the moon and listening to the yells, hoots and drumbeats of the frightened villagers. Everybody was scaring away the evil spirits with all the noise they could make. Then, as slowly as it had come, the shadow over the moon faded away. So also faded away the sounds of bells and drums. Soon all was quiet. Only a few dogs still barked.

"It's all over," said Fabian. "See, the moon is clear. Everybody is going to bed now. The evil spirits were frightened away."

Fabian's hut was dark. The boys crept into the sweat house and lay on their straw mats. As Fabian often slept in the sweat house, and Agustín often stayed all night with him, the boys knew they could talk a long time of the things they had seen on the mountain. Agustín told a story of the old days, but Fabian never heard the end of it. He was soon asleep.

CHAPTER SIX

GRINGOS

THE daily summer rains came and went. The maize grew. Now Fabian was daily in the fields with his father, piling dirt about the young plants and hoeing down weeds. Yet he still had time to play, to go to the village market, and to hoe his secret maize. One afternoon in late summer as the rain poured down from a leaden sky, Fabian was in the hut playing with Chichi. Mother was weaving a sash on her stick loom. Tsnuk was watching her. Suddenly Fabian saw an Indian and two pack burros stop under a huge laurel tree for shelter. Then he saw two strangers wearing black rain capes. They were gringos, like those he sometimes saw in the market. His heart jumped. Was it possible that Señor Gómez, the Mexican, and Señor Johnson were really coming to find the CITY UP YONDER as Quin had said?

"Mother, Mother," he cried, "look, there are strangers under that tree with two burros. They are gringos." Tsnuk ran to the door and stared. She was frightened of strangers. Mother only said, "Gringos," and went on with her weaving. "Gringos," echoed Chichi from her perch, blinking her sleepy eyes. Fabian watched the men trying to keep dry in the pouring rain. Soon they would be wet to the skin, he thought. One gringo had a black beard, the other a red beard. They MUST be Quin's friends.

"Mother," he whispered again, "it is raining so hard, let us ask them in where it is dry."

"But your father is away, Fabian, and won't be home for several days. Besides they are gringos," answered mother.

Then Fabian knew he HAD to tell his mother of Quin and how the gringos helped him when he had fallen on the trail that rainy morning so long ago. As he whispered the story to her quickly, his mother stared at him. She could hardly believe what he said. Just then the Indian came to the door and stood silently in the rain. He bowed politely and said in his local language, "The strangers grow wet. May we wait under your roof until the rain is over? The strangers do not know our language and are from afar."

Mother stared at him, still a little frightened, and then said, "Yes, enter." Seeing that she was afraid, the Indian added, "The President has sent them."

"Then tell them to come in until the rain stops," said mother.

As the strangers approached, Fabian's heart beat fast. He KNEW they were Quin's friends. They both looked kindly. As they entered the hut, they slipped their black rain capes from their shoulders and bowed politely to Mother, saying something to the

Indian who said, "The señores beg pardon for coming into your home, but it rains hard. When the rain is over they will depart. Do not fear."

He was so polite that Mother said, "Sit down, Señores, and rest. My husband is away. What seek you in this far-off place?"

Then Redbeard, who seemed to be the leader, said something to the Indian, for he replied, "We seek the CITY UP YONDER to dig for ancient things. The President wants us to do so. He hopes we may find things left by the people before us, the Mayan priests and kings. The last king of your race stood out against the Spanish invaders in the CITY UP YONDER." As he said this he unrolled a piece of white paper. Fabian saw on it a glittering golden circle and a bright red ribbon. There was writing on it too, but he could neither read nor write. "This says," continued Redbeard to the Indian who was named Lorenzo, "that we may dig and all that we may find at the CITY UP YONDER goes to the President." The Indian translated this and added, "I am the guide for these strangers."

Mother felt better now. She poured hot coffee into gourds and handed them to the strangers. The rain poured down and Chichi croaked sadly of her bad, bad cold. The Redbeard asked Fabian his name, and when the boy told it, a smile passed over his face. He said something to Lorenzo, who said quickly, "The señor says he met your brother Quin, in the Highlands. You do have a brother named Quin?"

"Yes," was all that Fabian could say, for all at once he knew that he would help dig on the mountain and become a friend to these kindly strangers. Redbeard spoke further to Lorenzo, for

the Indian said to Mother, "The señores wish to have a boy to help them on the mountain. Not only to guide them to the CITY UP YONDER but to stay with them. Do you think, Señora, that your son would do this for them? They will pay him well, and feed him well."

This was a hard thing for Mother to decide. She knew that when her husband came home he would be very angry with her for letting Fabian go with the gringos to dig in the haunted place. Yet she knew they had saved Quin from possible death and how good they had been to her dear son. She was torn between love of Quin and obedience to her husband. But at last she smiled at the Indian and said quietly, "Yes, Fabian may go with you just as soon as the rain stops. His father will be gone for some days. When he returns I will tell him you are friends."

Fabian stooped down and took his black and white shoulder bag from under his sleeping mat. He slipped his machete in his sash and stood ready. The rain stopped as suddenly as it had begun. In the bright rays of a late afternoon sun Fabian followed Lorenzo and the burros and his newly found friends toward the lake.

The weeks that followed were the most wonderful that Fabian had ever known. Every morning they dug about the great carved rocks of the CITY UP YONDER and near the ruined pyramids and fallen walls. When they found old objects Señor Johnson tied white tags on them. Gómez wrote something in a book. After it was written both men could read what had been written. Fabian learned more and more Spanish as the days went by. Before long he could talk with the strangers even when Lorenzo did not translate. Best of all were the evenings around the supper fire. Such strange foods they had to eat, foods from tin cans. Fabian ate and ate and as the days went by seemed to grow stronger and stronger. Sometimes Señor Johnson told Fabian about his own country far away. Señor Gómez loved to talk of the old days of kings and priests, both in Guatemala and in a place called Yucatán. Both men told Fabian of the beautiful buildings his forefathers had built, of the carved temples, handsome pyramids and good roads. They told him that priests sacrificed war prisoners upon stone altars. Sometimes he could not sleep at night, thinking of the stories the men told.

But in spite of daily digging, the explorers found little of value, only countless jade beads, and bits of broken pottery and one almost complete ceremonial jar.

"If we could only find a whole figure," sighed Señor Johnson, "perhaps a figure of the Corn Goddess or the God of Rain. Or a jade knife, or copper bells, or a nose ornament. Something beside just these beads, beads, beads and obsidian chips." He was growing discouraged. Then Fabian thought of the jade earplug lying in his bag and wondered if he should give it to them just to make

them happy. But the more he thought about this the more precious the earplug seemed.

One night he listened to Gómez and Johnson talking together in low voices. They thought he was asleep. Often he heard his name mentioned. He could not understand much of what they said for they spoke quietly. The next morning Lorenzo told him that Johnson had said Fabian should go to school. He learned fast. For Fabian had told him of the magic maize and had showed him his tiny field. They thought him a bright boy, who might some-day become a leader of his people. But Fabian could only think how hard it would be to change his father's hatred of schools and the gringos.

Late that afternoon as Lorenzo was digging carefully about a half-fallen pyramid, he suddenly cried, "Come, see what I have found."

The other ran to him. There lying in the palm of his brown hand was a lovely gray-green earplug, richly carved. Fabian stared. His heart beat fast. There lay the twin of his own treasure. The very same carving was upon both of them. It was carved by the same hand as the one he had found many months ago. As the three men smiled and laughed, so happy were they, Fabian pulled his bag from under his sleeping mat, and took out the earplug. Holding it up to Señor Johnson, he said, "Look, Señores, they are alike. Both carved alike by the same artist. See the winged serpent."

"Fabian," they exclaimed together, "where did you find this and when?"

Fabian looked up at them, truth shining in his brown eyes as he answered, "Many months ago, Señores, I found this. When we planted the magic maize my hand touched it. On that night when the moon died. I have carried it in my bag ever since with the jaguar teeth and the quetzal feathers. I did not know it was of much worth. I liked it. It was beautiful."

Señor Johnson held the two earplugs in his hand as he said, "Indeed it is as Fabian says. They are alike. We have never found a pair before. And so beautifully carved too. The man who carved these earplugs was an artist."

Then Gómez looked hard at Fabian. His eyes were no longer kind as he growled, "And, boy, why did you not show us this before, when we found nothing but beads and broken pieces of pottery. Tell me why?"

There were tears in Fabian's honest eyes as he explained again, "Indeed, Señor Gómez I meant no harm. REALLY I did

not know the jade was of such value. Here, I will give it to you, and I want nothing for it."

"Easy, easy, Gómez," said Señor Johnson gently. "The boy is telling the truth. I am sure you found this long ago, Fabian. I see it in your eyes." He placed his hand on the boy's shoulder. "They belong together, Señor," exclaimed Fabian. "They are as alike as the twin ear of maize that we kept on the altar at home. They are for the President," he whispered.

"Well, Fabian, you have really found a rare treasure. You will not give the earplug to us or to the President. We will buy it from you. This earplug will bring you and your family many quetzales. Your father need not fear for his crop. He will not need to go to the coffee field if his crop should fail. This earplug will take care of all of you. . . . And perhaps you can go to school, Fabian, if your father will permit it."

When Señor Johnson said this Fabian's heart jumped. He wanted to learn to read the black marks on the white paper that Señor Gómez wrote. Just then a heavy peal of thunder sounded below them. Far down on the slope of the volcano swept a gray torrent of rain as if a giant had turned on a heavenly faucet. Where that gray torrent fell the maize fields would be ruined. Fabian wondered if his father's field was safe. The violent gray plume fell near his father's maize, but he could not be sure.

"Now that we have found the earplug, we must pack and leave for the city," said Señor Johnson. "The President will be happy." Before leaving Fabian hoed about his fast-growing maize. Just to show to Father, he plucked a ripening ear and placed it in his bag. Two days later they started for the lower lands.

CHAPTER SEVEN

THE JADE EARPLUG

WHEN the party of explorers was halfway down the volcano, Fabian searched for his father's field. It was almost all washed away. The cloudburst had fallen just above it. Now a deep canyon ran through the field. On either side of the canyon the maize lay flat upon the ground.

"Poor Father," sighed the boy, tears in his eyes. "He prayed to the Wind Gods. He prayed to the Rain Gods. He gave them food. He sacrificed a turkey to the Gods on the Mountain. He put the sacred twine around his field. But in spite of all these things, the gods have deserted him. His maize is ruined. His field is gone. Perhaps we will go to the coffee plantation after all and pick coffee berries."

But the gringos said cheerfully, "Never mind, Fabian, it will be all right." As they approached the hut, Fabian whispered to Señor Johnson. "Wait outside until I see how Father feels. He may be very, very angry. He may not speak to you. He may think the gods have done this to his field because I went with you. See, outside the door lie the sacred images, even Santiago. That shows Father is very angry."

As the boy entered his own home, he saw Father huddled in a blanket in a dark corner, his eyes closed. He looked miserable. Chichi chirped, and Father opened his eyes. Then he saw Fabian.

"Oh, so you are back again, you and the gringos. And you went away without asking me."

"Yes Father, but Mother said I could go. The gringos were good to me. I have something wonderful to tell you."

"What could be wonderful now, stupid boy? Now that the field is gone. Now that we have nothing to eat. Now that we must pick coffee berries or starve?" growled Father.

"No, Father, we do not have to pick berries, even if the field is washed away. The gringos will tell you the good news."

"GRINGOS," spat Father. "When did gringos ever bring good news?"

"Wait, husband, be patient. Perhaps the boy is right," exclaimed Mother who was huddled near the fire.

Just then the three men walked slowly into the hut and took off their hats. They were very courteous. Father stared at them angrily. Mother said, "Sit, Señores, the boy says you bring good news. We have need of good news now."

Then Señor Johnson, understanding the fear of strangers

that lay in the hearts of all simple and downtrodden peoples, took from his pocket a flashlight and handed it to Father. When Fabian saw this marvelous gift in his father's hands, he knew things would be all right. Señor Johnson showed him where to press a place on the flashlight and suddenly a beam of brilliant light lit up the dark hut. Father smiled and shot the light into the far corners of the gloomy hut, frightening Chichi and making her cry like a baby.

Then Lorenzo said, "The Señor says the flashlight is yours, friend."

Father could hardly believe his good fortune. He completely forgot his visitors as he pushed the button on and off. Then Señor Gómez handed Mother two bright red combs for her hair. This made her even more friendly. She poured coffee for the guests. As they were drinking Señor Johnson spoke to Lorenzo. Finally Lorenzo said to Father, "We have been a long time on the volcano. Only two days ago we found a very fine jade earplug of the ancients. Then your son, who helped us a great deal, brought us an earplug he had found many months ago. They are twins. Your son's earplug is very valuable. You will see how valuable."

Then Señor Johnson laid on a stool a pile of silver coins. Father stared at him. "The President will be very glad. We now buy the jade earplug from your son. You see we give you many quetzales for it."

Father could scarcely believe his eyes. He had never seen so many coins in his life. How foolish are these strangers, he thought, to give us so many quetzales for just a little piece of old green stone one finds in the fields.

"These coins will pay for the ruined maize," continued

Lorenzo, translating the words of Señor Johnson. "No more will you need go to the coffee plantation. Not this year nor next year either. And if your son could go to school, it would be well for him and perhaps for your people. He learns fast. Already he speaks much Spanish."

Father said nothing. He was trying hard to understand, but too many things had happened all at once. He rose, went outdoors, picked up the sacred images, placed them on the altar. Then he knelt and closed his eyes. For some minutes he prayed to the Virgin Mary whose sweet face smiled down at him. He prayed to Santiago for understanding. After a while he rose, his eyes shining with faith, and said to the gringos, "This is too much for me to understand. But now I trust you. You are friends of the President, and so you are a friend of ours."

Father was watching the faces of the gringos so he did not see or hear Quin enter the hut, *cascate* on his back. When the elder brother saw the gringos, he thrust out his hand as his dark face broke into a smile. "Quin," cried Señor Johnson and Señor Gomez in one breath. They shook hands. Father stared.

"Oh, so you know these men?" he asked, suspiciously.

"Yes, I met them months ago on an old trail to a highland market. They saved my life. I lost my footing in the rain and they helped me. They fed me, and we became friends. They are good, Father."

Now Father's head was truly in a whirl. But when Chichi screamed, "Oh I got a cold, I got a cold," they all laughed together. Fabian felt at last that everybody was everybody else's friend.

This seemed to the Mayan boy the time to bring out his ear

of new maize. He took it from his bag and handed it to his father, as he said, "Look at this, Father."

Father took the ear of silky maize and saw the kernels, large and alike, as he asked, "Where did you get this, Fabian?"

"It is mine, Father, I grew it in my own field. I had twenty kernels of a new maize that came from afar. Quin gave it to me. I planted only one seed in each hole near the CITY UP YONDER, the night the moon died. Agustín helped me. Each kernel grew, Father, see, and now the maize is tall and strong. The Wind Gods and the Rain Gods guarded it well."

"But why did you not tell me of this before, Fabian?" asked Father sternly.

"Because I was afraid, Father. I was afraid you would not like this new seed. I was afraid you might throw it to the pigs when you learned that Quin gave it to me and that he got it from these strangers. But it is beautiful and strong."

"So it is," said Father thoughtfully. "And the kernels are one like the other."

"It is magic maize, Father, for Quin said in Mexico, where many Indians plant it, the people have more to eat than ever before."

"It is so, Señor," added Gómez.

"Can it be true?" said Father in a soft voice, his eyes full of wonder.

Then Lorenzo spoke, "The gringos say your son is a very bright boy for his years. They say he might become a leader of his people when he becomes a man. He is the seed of the future as the new maize is the seed of the future."

The candle burned brightly on the altar. Mother patted tortillas and slapped them on the smoking griddle. Father was silent, playing with his flashlight, and thinking as he looked at the pile of quetzales and the new maize. Then, as if the bright light of the sun had pierced a dark storm cloud, he stood up. Smiling, he walked toward the gringos, holding out his hand. "Even if you are strangers, and from afar, and not of my blood, Señores, you have saved us from the coffee plantation. And the boy may go to school if you and the President think he can really learn the new ways. I am too old to learn them. I cannot understand everything that has happened. But I trust you."

"Fabian will be a leader of his people some day," translated Lorenzo from Señor Johnson's words. "But first he must be wise. He must know the new as well as the old truths. We will return next year. Perhaps then you will try the new seed and learn for yourself."

Smiling, the three men walked toward their waiting burros. Fabian, Mother, Father and Quin stood in the doorway watching them go and waving to them as long as they could see them. Then Father placed his hand on Fabian's shoulder, and his arm around Quin, as he said, "It is beautiful maize, my sons."

"Yes, Father, it is beautiful maize."

And then Fabian knew that Quin was forgiven when Father said, "Let us go together, my sons, to the CITY UP YONDER on the volcano. We will see together the new maize, and how tall and beautiful it is." And then as Mother smiled and Chichi giggled, the three Indians walked out of the door into the sunshine.